The Inside Guide: FAMOUS NATIVE AMERICANS

Wilma Mankiller

By Jennifer Lombardo

Published in 2025 by Cavendish Square Publishing, LLC
2544 Clinton Street Buffalo, NY 14224

Copyright © 2025 by Cavendish Square Publishing, LLC

First Edition

No part of this publication may be reproduced, stored in a retrieval system, or transmitted in any form or by any means—electronic, mechanical, photocopying, recording, or otherwise—without the prior permission of the copyright owner. Request for permission should be addressed to Permissions, Cavendish Square Publishing, 2544 Clinton Street Buffalo, NY 14224. Tel (877) 980-4450; fax (877) 980-4454.

Website: cavendishsq.com

This publication represents the opinions and views of the author based on their personal experience, knowledge, and research. The information in this book serves as a general guide only. The author and publisher have used their best efforts in preparing this book and disclaim liability rising directly or indirectly from the use and application of this book.

All websites were available and accurate when this book was sent to press.

Library of Congress Cataloging-in-Publication Data

Names: Lombardo, Jennifer, author.
Title: Wilma Mankiller / Jennifer Lombardo.
Description: Buffalo, NY : Cavendish Square Publishing, [2025] | Series: The inside guide: Famous native Americans | Includes bibliographical references and index.
Identifiers: LCCN 2024006585 | ISBN 9781502671196 (library binding) | ISBN 9781502671189 (paperback) | ISBN 9781502671202 (ebook)
Subjects: LCSH: Mankiller, Wilma, 1945-2010–Juvenile literature. | Cherokee Indians–Biography–Juvenile literature. | LCGFT: Biographies.
Classification: LCC E99.C5 L643 2025 | DDC 973.04/975570092 [B]–dc23/eng/20240320
LC record available at https://lccn.loc.gov/2024006585

Editor: Jennifer Lombardo
Copyeditor: Jill Keppeler
Designer: Deanna Lepovich

The photographs in this book are used by permission and through the courtesy of: Cover Everett Collection Inc/Alamy Stock Photo; p. 4 PhotoTrippingAmerica/Shutterstock.com; p. 6 randy andy/Shutterstock.com; p. 7 JNix/Shutterstock.com; p. 9 Don Pablo/Shutterstock.com; p. 10 Forty3Zero/Shutterstock.com; p. 12 f11photo/Shutterstock.com; p. 13 jdwfoto/Shutterstock.com; p. 15 WENN Rights Ltd/Alamy Stock Photo; p. 16 Assignment- 48-DPA-07-25-07 K DOI-U Pathways) Participants in the Pathways to Leadership management training program, (for Bureau of indian Affairs (BIA) and Office of the Special T - DPLA -383a990d86b15fee1c913462c6dcd71a/Wikimedia Commons; pp. 19, 21, 22 (main), 28 (right) Buddy Mays/Alamy Stock Photo; p. 20 Dee Browning/Shutterstock.com; p. 22 (inset) Dennis MacDonald/Shutterstock.com; p. 24 xpixel/Shutterstock.com; p. 25 Teresa Otto/Shutterstock.com; p. 26 MattRuffmanPhotography/Shutterstock.com; p. 28 (left) Mirza Kadic/Shutterstock.com; p. 29 (left) Michael Vi/Shutterstock.com; p. 29 (right) Alessia Pierdomenico/Shutterstock.com.

Some of the images in this book illustrate individuals who are models. The depictions do not imply actual situations or events.

CPSIA compliance information: Batch #CSCSQ25: For further information contact Cavendish Square Publishing LLC at 1-877-980-4450.

Printed in the United States of America

CONTENTS

Chapter One: 5
  Early Life

Chapter Two: 11
  Social Movements

Chapter Three: 17
  Big Accomplishments

Chapter Four: 23
  Honored and Remembered

Think About It! 28

Timeline 29

Glossary 30

Find Out More 31

Index 32

Shown here is the original capitol building in Tahlequah, Oklahoma. Today, the building houses the Cherokee National History Museum.

EARLY LIFE

Chapter One

Wilma Mankiller was born in 1945 in Tahlequah, Oklahoma. This is the capital city of the Cherokee Nation. She was the 6th of 11 children. When she was growing up, Mankiller and her family did not have electricity, indoor plumbing, or a telephone. However, she has stated in interviews that the lack of these things did not make her feel poor.

From Oklahoma to California

In 1956, when Mankiller was 11 years old, her family moved to San Francisco, California. That year, the U.S. government had passed a law called the Indian Relocation Act. The government said the law was meant to help Native Americans get jobs in big cities. Under the act, the government paid the moving costs for Mankiller's family, and her father received free job training in San Francisco.

Fast Fact
"Mankiller," or "Asgaya-dihi" in Cherokee, is a traditional Cherokee military rank. A similar English name might be Wilma Major.

The Mankiller family was forced to move to San Francisco, shown here, when Wilma was a child.

Although the Indian Relocation Act sounded nice, it was not actually a nice thing for the government to do. With federal support taken away if they stayed home, Mankiller's family and many others had no choice but to move. The law was one

Fast Fact

Mankiller hated San Francisco so much that she saved her babysitting money and bought a bus ticket to her grandparents' house in Riverbank, California. Her parents brought her home, but after she did this four more times, they agreed to let her stay in Riverbank for a year.

THE TRAIL OF TEARS

The Cherokee Nation did not start out in Oklahoma. The traditional home of the Cherokee was in and around what are now the states of North Carolina, Tennessee, Georgia, and Alabama. In the 1830s, the U.S. government began telling the Cherokee and several other Native American nations, including the Chocktaw and Creek, that they would need to move to Oklahoma.

Many Native Americans ignored the order. In 1838, the U.S. Army came in to enforce it. They marched the Native Americans on foot from their homelands to Oklahoma. Thousands died along the way, and many more became sick or hurt, giving this **ethnic cleansing** event and the route itself the name "The Trail of Tears."

This statue commemorating, or remembering, the Trail of Tears stands outside the Trail of Tears Memorial and Museum in Pulaski, Tennessee.

of several **termination** acts the U.S. government passed between 1946 and 1970. These acts disbanded, or split up, many Native American groups and took away the money they had been promised by the government under previous laws. It also allowed the government to sell reservation land—land that had been promised to Native Americans by various treaties in the 1700s and 1800s—and close some schools and health clinics on the land that was left.

The government's goal in passing these laws was to force Native Americans to **assimilate** to white culture, or ways of life, and to weaken the power of independent tribes. It took away financial support from Native American communities and forced Native Americans to move away from the people and places they had cultural ties to. Mankiller called her family's move "my own little Trail of Tears."

Activism Starts at Home

In San Francisco, the Mankillers lived in a housing project—a neighborhood owned by the government. Wilma's father, Charley, worked in a warehouse. He soon became a union organizer, working to create a group that could help his fellow warehouse workers get better pay and better working conditions. He was also active in the Indian rights movement that was taking place around this time. His social **activism** strongly influenced Wilma when she was young.

Fast Fact
Charley Mankiller's family originally came from Tennessee. They were forced to relocate to Oklahoma on the Trail of Tears.

Warehouse work is hard on the body.
Unions have helped make this work safer.

Most people are familiar with the Black civil rights movement of the 1960s. However, there were many other civil rights movements going on at the same time that were not as widely talked about.

SOCIAL MOVEMENTS

Chapter Two

The 1960s were a time of social change in many different areas. Black people, women, Native Americans, and other groups were speaking out, getting organized, and demanding respect. They wanted the same rights white men had. The **feminist** and Native American movements had a strong influence on Mankiller.

Alcatraz

In 1969, a group of Native American activists took over Alcatraz Island in San Francisco. The occupiers had a few goals in mind. They wanted the deed, or legal right, to the island, which had been occupied by Native people for thousands of years before it became part of the United States. They wanted to create a Native American university, museum, and cultural center on the island. Ultimately, they wanted to show the world that Native Americans needed **self-determination**.

Seeing this on the news was a wake-up call for Mankiller. She

> **Fast Fact**
> Intersectionality is the idea that the same person can experience multiple kinds of **oppression**. Mankiller, a woman and a Native American, experienced sexism and racism at the same time.

realized that there was a lot of work to be done to help Native Americans let non-Natives know what was happening to them. She began her own social activism

The U.S. government ran a prison on Alcatraz Island from 1907 to 1963.

work in California, helping local Native communities. She became the director of Oakland's Native American Youth Center, helping young adults. Many of them were homeless because of the high rate of poverty in urban, or city, Native American communities.

People often think of Native Americans as living only on reservations. However, many Native American people today live and work in cities. Shown here are Native people selling handmade items at a craft fair in the city of Santa Fe, New Mexico.

> ### Fast Fact
> Mankiller was already connected to San Francisco's Native American community by 1969. She had joined the Indian Center of San Francisco as a teen and spent a lot of time there. However, the Alcatraz occupation marked the start of her activism.

MARRIED AND DIVORCED

In 1963, Mankiller married a man she had met while they were both studying at San Francisco State College. His name was Hector Hugo Olaya de Bardi. By 1966, they had two daughters, and Wilma decided to be a stay-at-home mother.

When the Alcatraz occupation happened, Mankiller wanted to join the activists. Her husband said she was not allowed. She sent money to the activists, but she really wanted to take a more active role. De Bardi did not support her activism and wanted her to continue to stay at home. In 1974, the couple divorced, and Mankiller moved back to Oklahoma with her children soon after.

Mankiller also worked with the Pit River Tribe of California as it fought a legal battle. The Pacific Gas and Electric Company owned millions of acres of Pit River land, which had been taken from the tribe unfairly in the 1800s. The tribe wanted the company to either give the land back or give the tribe fair payment for it. The battle taught Mankiller a lot about Native Americans' legal rights. These lessons helped her later in life, when she became the chief of the Cherokee Nation.

Activism in Oklahoma

Mankiller did not stop **advocating** for her people when she left San Francisco. Back in Oklahoma, she started working to improve living conditions for Cherokee communities. In 1981, she created the Community Development Department for the Cherokee Nation. Her first project in this role was in Bell, Oklahoma, in a small Cherokee community.

The Cherokee families living in Bell had no running water and few jobs. Their living conditions made many of them feel hopeless. Mankiller brought the community together to make a change. She organized volunteers to build a water system. They worked so well together that the project was completed in only 14 months. The sense of accomplishment the community felt helped raise their spirits. Mankiller had given them hope and empowered them.

Fast Fact

The Bell water project inspired a 2013 movie called *The Cherokee Word for Water*. Charlie Soap helped direct it. Native American actress and activist Kimberly Guerrero played Mankiller.

Mankiller met her second husband, Charlie Soap, who is shown here, while she was working on the Bell project. They were married in 1986.

Ross Swimmer (*right*) told Wilma Mankiller he wanted her to be his deputy chief because she cared about the Cherokee community and was honest with money.

BIG ACCOMPLISHMENTS

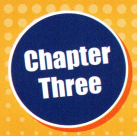

Chapter Three

Mankiller's work in Bell got her noticed by Cherokee Principal Chief Ross Swimmer. In 1983, he asked her to be his deputy chief when he ran for reelection. Mankiller agreed, and Swimmer won. When he stepped down from the position in 1985 to work for the U.S. government, Mankiller became principal chief—the first woman to ever hold this role.

From Deputy to Principal

Mankiller first became principal chief because it was the duty of the deputy chief to take over if the principal chief could not or would not continue to do the job. She finished the term Swimmer had been elected to, then ran for principal chief herself. The Cherokee people liked her enough to elect her in 1987 and again in 1991.

Mankiller quickly proved that she was the best person for the job. As principal chief, she used what she had learned from the Alcatraz activists and the Pit River Tribe to help make

Fast Fact
The principal chief is like the president of the Cherokee Nation. The deputy chief is like the vice president.

SEXISM AT HOME

The feminist movement was still ongoing in the 1980s, and as a woman, Mankiller had to deal with sexism even from her own people. The way Cherokee elections worked in the 1980s, the person running for principal chief picked a group, or slate, of 16 people to fill the available government positions. People voted for the entire slate.

When Swimmer picked Mankiller as his deputy chief, the rest of his slate said they would quit. They did not like that she was a woman or that she was part of the Democratic Party when they were Republicans—members of a different political party. Swimmer stood by his decision even when most of the slate followed through with their threat. His former deputy chief ran against him for principal chief, but Swimmer and Mankiller won.

the Cherokee Nation even better than it already was. She doubled the community's budget, and she made the Cherokee Nation the first Native American group to make a self-governance compact with the United States. This was an agreement that allowed the Cherokee to govern themselves independent of the U.S. government.

Fast Fact

The self-governance compact granted the Cherokee their own law enforcement and court system instead of forcing them to work with the ones that reported to the U.S. government.

This picture of Mankiller was taken in 1986, a year after she took over Swimmer's position as principal chief.

Improving Health

Another of Mankiller's accomplishments was getting health clinics built on Cherokee lands. Building health clinics that were close and easy to get to, both in an emergency and for regular checkups, did a lot to improve the overall health of the community. Mankiller was very proud of that part of her work.

Although people had been unsure of her at first, Mankiller quickly became popular and respected, both inside and outside the Cherokee community. When someone said "Wilma," everyone knew who they

This health center in Stilwell, Oklahoma, is named after Mankiller to honor her work in getting such clinics built.

Fast Fact

Mankiller also improved education and housing in Cherokee communities while she served as principal chief.

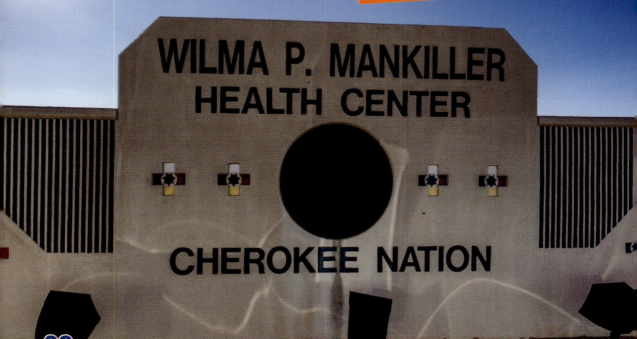

were talking about. She was good at talking to people, listening to their concerns, and addressing those concerns before they turned into big problems.

Many people were sad when Mankiller decided not to run for chief again in 1995. However, they were happy to know that she was not planning to stop working for the community. Until her death in 2010, she continued to speak up for social justice, especially for Native Americans and women.

Mankiller is shown here next to a statue of John Ross, the longest-running principal chief of the Cherokee Nation.

In 1998, President Bill Clinton awarded Mankiller the Presidential Medal of Freedom. This is the highest honor the U.S. government can give to a civilian.

HONORED AND REMEMBERED

Chapter Four

Mankiller was **dedicated** to her work serving the Cherokee Nation. In 1990, she was **hospitalized** several times and had a kidney transplant. However, this did not stop her from running for principal chief again the following year, when she won 82 percent of the votes. In 2010, when she was 64 years old, Wilma Mankiller died of pancreatic cancer. She was honored in many ways both before and after her death.

A New Quarter

Up until the 2000s, most of the people on American money have been men. The U.S. Mint, which makes and issues American money, has made more of an effort in recent years to showcase important women. The American Women Quarters Program, which was started in 2022 and is set to run until 2025, puts American women who made important contributions to history on the backs of some quarter coins.

Fast Fact

Pancreatic cancer affects the pancreas. This organ helps us digest food and keep our blood sugar stable.

23

Wilma Mankiller is one of 20 important American women who are being honored with the American Women Quarters Program.

Fast Fact
George Washington's wife, Martha Washington, was pictured on the back of the $1 bill in the 1800s.

Each year, five new quarters are made, featuring five different women. Mankiller's quarter was issued in 2022, along with those of Maya Angelou, a writer, performer, and activist; Sally Ride, a scientist and the first female astronaut to go to space; Nina Otera-Warren, a **suffragist** and first female superintendent of public schools in Santa Fe, New Mexico; and Anna May Wong, the first Chinese American Hollywood actress.

Mankiller Barbie

Mankiller was also honored by the company Mattel as part of its Inspiring Women series of Barbie dolls. Mankiller is shown wearing a traditional Cherokee ribbon skirt and black shoes and is holding a

Ribbon skirts such as these have been adopted by women of all Native American groups. The skirt is seen as an item of clothing that unites all Native American women, no matter where they come from.

BARBIE CONTROVERSY

There was some controversy, or disagreement, about the Wilma Mankiller Barbie. Some people were not very happy about how the doll turned out. They said Mattel did not do enough research when it was creating the doll and its packaging. For example, the package included the word "Cherokee" in the Cherokee syllabary, or written language. However, Mattel used the wrong symbols, so the box actually says "chicken" instead. Some people were also upset about the fact that the doll's face looks more like a regular Barbie than like Mankiller.

Mankiller's daughter Felicia Olaya has mixed feelings about the Barbie. On the one hand, she said, she likes that her mother is being honored in a way little girls can connect with. On the other, she is not sure Mankiller would have liked to be celebrated as a Barbie. Olaya said her mother was very humble and did not like to brag about her accomplishments.

This is an example of the Cherokee syllabary, which was created by a man named Sequoyah in the early 1800s.

> **Fast Fact**
> The ribbons a woman chooses to put on her skirt tell a story. The colors, styles, lengths, and more each have a specific meaning.

basket. Mattel worked with Charlie Soap and Mankiller's friend Kristina Kiehl to create the doll. Some people felt that the doll was a wonderful way to honor and remember such an important woman. Principal Chief Chuck Hoskin Jr. said he was happy that his daughter and other Native girls had a Barbie to represent them and show them that they can make a difference in the world.

In December 2023, when the Barbie was released, the Cherokee Nation held a **ceremony** to honor Mankiller and her achievements. Many people spoke fondly about Mankiller. They said she was cheerful, hardworking, and made a big difference in many people's lives. Although Mankiller herself is gone, her presence is still felt in Tahlequah, and the work she set in motion is being carried on by others today.

THINK ABOUT IT!

1. Why do you think the U.S. government wanted to force Native Americans to assimilate?
2. What other forms of intersectional oppression can you think of?
3. What do you think Mankiller's biggest accomplishment was as principal chief?
4. Do you think a Barbie was a good way to honor Mankiller? Why or why not?

TIMELINE

Wilma Mankiller's Life

1945
Wilma Mankiller is born.

1956
Mankiller moves to San Francisco.

1969
She is inspired by Alcatraz occupation.

1981
Mankiller establishes Cherokee Nation's Community Development Department.

1985
Mankiller becomes first female chief of the Cherokee Nation.

2010
Mankiller dies.

World Events

1945
The Nuremberg Trials for Nazi war criminals begin.

1949
Mao Zedong makes China a Communist country.

1969
Neil Armstrong walks on the moon.

1979
Iranian Revolution puts Ayatollah Khomeini in charge.

1989
The Berlin Wall falls.

1994
Nelson Mandela is elected South Africa's first Black president.

GLOSSARY

activism: Acting strongly in support of or against an issue.

advocate: To argue for or support a cause or policy.

assimilate: To make a thing or person exactly like the others around it.

ceremony: A formal act or series of acts performed in some regular way.

civilian: A person who is not part of the military.

dedicated: Committed to a goal or way of life.

ethnic cleansing: The act of killing, imprisoning, or forcibly relocating a minority group.

feminist: A person who believes in and fights for gender equality.

hospitalize: To check into a hospital for treatment that lasts more than one day.

oppression: Cruel or unfair use of power over others.

self-determination: The ability of a person or group to govern themselves.

suffragist: A person who fights for a certain group's right to vote.

termination: Sudden ending.

traditional: Based on custom.

FIND OUT MORE

Books
Beason, Jimmy, and Amanda Lenz. *Native Americans in History: A History Book for Kids*. Emeryville, CA: Rockridge Press, 2021.

Bruchac, Joseph. *Voices of the People*. New York, NY: Reycraft Books, 2022.

Sorrell, Traci, and Gillian Flint. *Wilma Mankiller*. New York, NY: Philomel Books, 2022.

Websites
Kiddle: Wilma Mankiller Facts for Kids
kids.kiddle.co/Wilma_Mankiller
Read more about Mankiller's amazing life.

KidsKonnect: Cherokee History Facts
kidskonnect.com/history/cherokee
Learn more about the past and present of the Cherokee Nation.

Native Land
native-land.ca
This interactive map shows the traditional lands of Indigenous, or Native, cultures around the world. Find out whose land you're living on today.

Publisher's note to educators and parents: Our editors have carefully reviewed these websites to ensure that they are suitable for students. Many websites change frequently, however, and we cannot guarantee that a site's future contents will continue to meet our high standards of quality and educational value. Be advised that students should be closely supervised whenever they access the internet.

INDEX

A
Alcatraz Island, 11, 12, 13, 14, 17
American Women Quarters Program, 23, 24

B
Barbie, 25, 26, 27
Bell water system project, 15, 17

C
Cherokee, 4, 5, 7, 14, 15, 16, 17, 18, 20, 21, 23, 25, 26, 27

F
family, 5, 6, 8, 14, 15, 26

I
Indian Relocation Act, 5, 6
Indian rights movement, 8, 10, 11

O
Oklahoma, 4, 5, 7, 8, 14, 15, 20

P
Pit River Tribe, 14, 17
Presidential Medal of Freedom, 22

S
San Francisco, 5, 6, 8, 11, 13, 14
Swimmer, Ross, 16, 17, 18, 19

T
Tahlequah, 4, 5, 27
Trail of Tears, 7, 8